THE HARP THAT ITSELF SINGS

THE HARP THAT ITSELF SINGS

poems

Laura Williams

atmosphere press

© 2024 Laura Williams

Published by Atmosphere Press

Cover design by Ronaldo Alves

No part of this book may be reproduced without permission from the author except in brief quotations and in reviews.

Atmospherepress.com

For my niblings—love y'all, kiddos.

CONTENTS

Veritas	1
Wolves' Tale	2
The Pale Crone's Smile	
Transformation	15
Woman in the Moon	16
To the Fairest	18
Monster	19
Weaving	20
Tempest in a Teacup (Don't Wake the Sleeping Ones)	22
Flight	24
Retribution	25
The Pale Crone's Smile	26
Patriarch	28
After Troy	29
Gifting	31
Pomegranate Queen	32
Sacrificial	33
Wanderer	35
Reign	36
Shoulders	37
Shadows Eternal	38
Rubies & Roses	
Hunger	41
Dreamer	42
Ocean Calling	43
Stepsister	47

Bargaining	48
Little Red	49
Curséd	50
The Tragedy of Snow White, in 7 Acts	51
Rubies & Roses	54
They Do Not Speak of After	56
Advice to a Widower	57
Dark and Fair	58
Crying Wolf	61
A Fairy's Tale	63
Fireplace	65
Escapism	68
To the Sea	70
The Twilight Kingdom	71
Petals and Jewels	74
Ignite	75
The Truth of Fairies	77

Exeunt

Deify	81

Veritas

You know, the true fairy tales rarely had a happy ending.
It's forgotten, these days, how the stories were bloody
and grim, tragedies of Greek proportions. Who could remember,
with Disney-fluff and kid books, bedtime stories of kings,
princesses, magical bumbling godmothers who always grant the wish?

In fact, Snow White's mother was the one who wanted her
heart and the poor dear died three (or was it four,
or five?) times. The prince raped Sleeping Beauty as she slept
and she woke to her twin children feeding at her breast.
Cinderella's stepsisters sawed off their feet to fit in the slipper—
Have you never heard of what happened after 'happily ever after'?

Rapunzel's boy lost his eyes, while Snow White's stepmother (if you
want to update the tale) danced herself to death at the sweet
princess's wedding on burning shoes. Hansel and Gretel were
cooked to be eaten and children don't get happy endings.

The dear little mermaid died as the handsome prince
kissed another; the sweet fish-girl became seafoam or clouddust,
something ephemeral—her sisters all mourned, wept,
screamed. There are so few happy endings, so why all the lies?
Why tell children that Goldilocks didn't get eaten,
not mention Prince Charming sprawled dead on the floor?

Oh, that's right—These stories are naught but children's tales
now, and children are innocent weaklings too young
to know the truth because of how ugly it is:
There is no happily ever after,
no riding into the sunset on a noble steed—
the sun would scorch everyone, anyway.

Wolves' Tale

[i]

Proclaims the minstrel:
   "A marvel I bring! The harp that itself sings!"

                                        Sings the harp pale as bone,
                                    strung by fine golden strings
                                            in a fragile, crooning,
                                                young girl's voice:

> *From the king I ran*
> *Along the shore of the*
> *Wide and rushing River Red*
> *Drowned I was so that*
> *My innocence I kept*

[ii]

Mourns the ocean:
Youngest daughter of the king
Away to the sun you flee
Lost on the shore so lonely
In our waters can no human breathe

                          Chortles the witch:
"Now, dear king,
with you distracted,
I shall myself avenge."

[iii]

Coughs the fairy:
  "A sip of water, dearie?"

                                          Croaks the fairy:
                                          "A sip of water, dearie?"

The first sister (younger, fairer, sweeter)
using her own ladle to scoop and offer the water:
  "Of course, Grandmother."

                            The second sister (older, plainer, bitter)
                                    impatient and a bit bewildered:
                      "This is our well, crone. Take your leave."

Answers the blessed sister:
  "Of$_{\text{(violet petal)}}$ course$_{\text{(opal)}}$, Your$_{\text{(daisy petal)}}$ Highness$_{\text{(pearl)}}$."

                                        Speaks the cursed sister:
                                                        "..."

[iv]

Wonders the seventh wife:
>This key, the smallest key, the golden key
>Oh, in my dreams it does bleed
>Drop by sinister drop, to pool at my feet
>This key, how can it cause
>Footprints to follow me down the halls?
>I wake with a scream in my throat and
>This small key, this golden key, clutched in my hand

>>The key:
>>Slides easily into the lock.
>>The knob:
>>Does not even turn.
>>The door:
>>Opens.

Weeps the seventh wife:
>Oh, my sisters, what has he done to you?
>Oh, my sisters, only your skulls remain
>In this blood-soaked hell hidden in my home
>Oh, my sisters, placed on the walls
>Like trophies, all six of you
>Were you commanded to never open the door?
>Did the key haunt you until you disobeyed?
>Oh, my sisters, can I escape this fate?

[v]

Flirts the queen
in her marriage bed with the king,
holding out an apple red as blood:
"I went walking in the fruit garden.
I saw this and it reminded me of you.
Eat it with me. Let it symbolize
our love, shared and shared alike."

                The queen,
          crown white as snow on her hair,
       smile red as blood, gown black as ebony:
           "Good people of this realm,
       though we mourn my beloved husband
         and my darling stepdaughter,
           I make a solemn oath.
    Until a suitable heir of the royal bloodline is found,
      I shall do my utmost to honor my husband
     by ruling as fairly and as strongly as I can."

[vi]

Brother:
  "Follow closely! This is
    surely the pathway home!
      Father is just beyond the wood!"

>Sister:
>"But what of Stepmother?"

Brother has no answer,
clutching Sister's hand even tighter.

>Welcomes the old woman:
>"Oh, children, come in, come in!
>You must be tired and cold.
>Here, sit by the fire.
>Have some soup
>to warm your bones."

Shouts Brother,
waking in a cage of bone:
  "Sister! Wake! Run!"

>Muses the old woman
>(in truth a witch):
>"Dear girl, do you want
>to leave your brother here
>alone but for me and the bones?"

Sings Sister,
weeping but obedient:

    Here I sweep, there I mop
    For dinner I dice the onions
    For breakfast I slice the ham
    And always I feel her eyes on me
    While brother and I do plan

>Cackles the witch:
>"Eat, boy, and grow plump
>for the meat shall be tender."

[vii]

                      Pronounces Godmother:
                    "To the ball you shall go!"

The servant girl
twirling around the floor
the prince's hands firm on her hips:

    Godmother, your magic gleams
    Diamonds pearls sparkling on my shining gown
    The silver tiara on my dark hair
    My lips painted such a brilliant red

                    Strikes the clock:
                    quarter 'til.

The servant girl:
    Strike as you like, master clock, tick tock tick tock
    But the magic shall not fade!
    My silly sister will waste away
    while the magic works exactly as I say!

                    Strikes the clock:
                    midnight.

Implores the prince,
walking in the garden
hand-in-hand with the servant girl:
"Become my wife, please."

                  Sings the newly-wed princess:

    Never will I return, Stepmother
    To my father's house on the edge of town
    Do you mourn my silly sister?
    Do you finally regret all you've done
    Now that I stand here, now that I've won?
    I kiss my husband, the future king
    And a golden tiara on my head gleams
    I kiss my husband and soon, Stepmother
    Soon, Godmother, I shall be queen

Murmurs Godmother:
    "There shall be a price."

                    Answers the queen:
                    "I'm prepared to pay it,
                    no matter the lives it costs."

[viii]

Sings the princess:
        Locked in this tower
    For my safety, for the good of a realm
        I've never once seen
  Magically, every morn and every eve
   A sumptuous meal appears for me
   And every time it's roast duck—
    Do you know how many times
    You can eat the same thing
 Before it becomes ash in your mouth?
  Magically, every eve there appears
A tub of warm water, soap, and a cloth
   And every morn and every eve
    I study the magic as it works
    For I've nothing else to do.
  And though it takes centuries
Finally, I weave a rope from the bedclothes
From my dresses, from even my cursed hair
   And with everything I've learned
I strengthen this rope with a spell of my own
With my will and blood and utter desperation

                    Proclaims the princess:
                    "I've climbed down the side
                    of that tower, and I'll see them
                    dead ere they cage me again."

Says the fisherman:
   "Yes, I've hidden your skin.
   I love your beauty—
   Be my wife."

                                   Answers the selkie:
                                  "I've no other choice
                                       but to say yes."

Says the selkie's daughter:
"Mother, look what I've found!"

                                  Commands the selkie:
                                  "Do not tell your father."

Sings the ocean:
         Daughter, you've waited and you've earned
        Daughter, reclaim what is yours and come home

                                  Murmurs the selkie:
                                  "Husband, wake. I've a gift."

Croons the selkie:
                For years I have waited
          And now I cannot wait a moment more
             I'll kiss you this final time
         First with my lips and then with this blade

                                    Call the selkies:
             Don't leave your skin on land
              We caution our daughters.
               Don't trust in landfolk
                We warn our sons.
           No one will fight for you
              We tell our children
           You must fight for yourself

[x]

Sings the cook:
>Oh daughter, daughter,
>When will I be blessed with your laughter?
>When will I have a babe to hold?
>How much longer must I wait
>How much longer must I weep and toil?

>>Instructs the fairy:
>>"Three days hence,
>>on the night
>>of the new moon,
>>drink the essence
>>of rose petals,
>>plucked from the bush
>>beside a fairy ring,
>>and seasoned with
>>a virgin's moonblood.
>>You shall have
>>a fierce child."

Sings the cook:
>She's born on a night of no moon at all
>My longed-for daughter
>And wolves howl outside of town when she cries
>She's always hungry, this girl-child of mine
>Her eyes so bright, her smile so sharp
>But oh, I love her so

>>Proclaims the fairy
>>and the witch
>>and Magic itself:
>>"There is a cost to be paid.
>>She shall be our blessing—
>>And she shall be our curse."

The Pale Crone's Smile

Transformation

Her island—a paradise, a trap, a cage.
Her captives, her pets, feast to glut her magic,
    to power her youth and immortality.
They cry, the sailors and pirates,
they beg and plead as their bones crack,
    their muscles constrict and contract,
    their bodies twist and change and break.
Her magic consumes their spirits and
eventually, she bodily feeds on their flesh.
Her island is her paradise, her eternal home—
    it began a prison, her punishment,
but as she transforms the sailors
                  pirates
                      shipwrecked fools
who crash on her shores,
she transforms her prison into her paradise.

Woman in the Moon

The night, empty sky:
Dark void.
Endless.
Vast lack of light.

Little lives
Toddling, trudging,
Knees scraped, feet bruised.

Sun sets, day rests—
No light, no sight.
Stare at the sky.

Little lives pray—
> *we cannot see*
> *help us please*
> *we cannot survive the night*

Daughter of the sun,
In her palace on
The other side of the sky,
Hears the prayers
Of the little lives.

From her garden's pool
She scoops a handful of water,
Fashions a small pale globe.
She steps into the vast void
To set the globe of water
In the little lives' sky.

Light—pale, kind
To ease the sleep of the little lives.
The sky no longer empty,
Dark void, vast.
Little lives stare,

See the handprint
Of the daughter of the sun
On the face of the moon.

To the Fairest

Fair Helen, the goddess says, smiling, *most beautiful daughter of Zeus.*

Helen stares at her, knowing her for who she is at a glance. *Milady*, she replies, inclining her head.

Aphrodite's smile only widens. *A prince comes to your shores. He will love you, and you will love him.*

Helen lifts her chin. *I have a husband*, she says, *and he is already a king.* Aphrodite raises an eyebrow. *You belong to Paris, little sister*, she says, the words ringing absolutely. *Thus I have commanded and so shall you obey.*

She's gone, leaving Helen alone in the room—but then Helen wakes up to birds calling and bright sunlight. She wants to believe it was just a dream. She knows it wasn't.

Weeks pass before the foreign princes arrive, honorable Hector and beautiful Paris. And Helen loves him from the first time she sees his eyes.

She smiles at him, wanting to cry.

Monster

Here is what they never tell you
when you're a monster:
    You're always dangerous.
    Asleep, awake,
    happy, frightened, or sad,
you are a threat
because you were born a monster.

Here is something else they never tell you:
    Monsters are not born.
    Monsters are made.
You are someone's choice.
        You are someone's *fault*.

Weaving

I. Threads

Never again, my sister, will
your hands spin beauty from
cloth for our eyes to dazzle on,
our dreaming yet to come.

You challenged a goddess, my
clever sister, to dare
in your pride, and then to compound
the folly, you laid bare

divine indiscretions for our
mortal eyes to see and
to shame the holy ones upon
the mountain where they stand.

Ten fingers, hands once so clever—
You wove simple threads to
such plain beauty and instead of
giving in, you stood true.

You spin still, my clever, foolish
sister, once so proud, so
determined to prove your worth.
You spin still, brought so low.

Are you yet content, Arachne?
Here, amidst your webs,
woven in the wild with naught to
prove, as a tide does ebb?

II. Arachne, as she spins

Eight legs, each can spin.
Before, I had only two hands.
I, proven to be the best by a goddess's rage—
I believe, from the center of my beautiful web,
This punishment an unknowingly given gift.

Tempest in a Teacup (Don't Wake the Sleeping Ones)

There are some beasts so big no cage in the world could contain them. They shrug their shoulders and mountains quake; they yawn and hurricanes swirl in the ocean; they sleep and countries form on their spines.

The Great Ones wake and the world shudders; the Great Ones stretch and the world crumbles.

She blinks; her (*arms?*) are chained to each other at the (*wrists?*), her legs at the ankles (*what words are these, what language? how does she know it—how does she **know**?*), and there are men glaring at her over the mouths of weapons she has never before seen.

"Who are you?" one of them demands.

How long has she slept? How did she come to be in this (*body*)?

She blinks at the shackles, at the man who demands an answer, and then she **reaches**—*oh*, she thinks, *oh, you clever little things.*

She laughs.

They are scattered over the worlds, the Great Ones, separated for the first time since they slept. Everything is out of balance; they should not be awake yet, not for long millennia. She should still be spread out with the (*Alps*) along her back.

But here she is, locked away in a dark room, angry little things demanding to know how she appeared in their inner sanctum.

She does not answer, of course, shackled hand and foot, hungry and hurt.

Some things were not meant to be caged. Some things cannot be contained. She is a Great One no matter her form. She inhales and the temperature drops; she exhales and the bindings on her body shatter.

She rises to her (*feet*) and whirlwinds fill the air.

She steps into sunlight, *reaching* again—a sister to the east, and a brother to the north... the only ones here on this tiny little planet.

They should not be awake. They are, nonetheless. She laughs, stretching her frail body just to feel the tremor all the way into the core of the earth.

Flight

father, father, the boy cries

will the sky remember?
clouds seek to reach, to catch, to hold
still down he plummets
wings melting and burning
skin sizzling as he screams

father, father

the ocean waits
ravenous, lustful,
wide and deep,
waves cresting like teeth,
to devour, consume,
keep

father, father

the wings that failed to keep him in the sky
drag him under the water
gagging on ocean even as ocean swallows him whole

father, father

sought to fly only to fall
perhaps humans were never meant
to soar on wings into the sky

my son, my son, weeps the father, still aloft on high,
whyever did i teach you to fly?

the sky remembers
what the ocean devours

Retribution

This world shall be hers
and everything in it
Whether she poisons
    gowns
    crowns
the very throne—
All will kneel before her
    feel the bite
        the sting
        the certainty of her grip
            around the realm
                the sky
                the ocean
First this puny little palace
Then the gods who scorned her
as she takes   Olympus
             the tempestuous children
                    who think they rule there

The Pale Crone's Smile

"Do you think they'd believe, if you told them?" the dark handmaiden asks, glancing up from the queen's hem. The thread is fraying; it is time to summon a seamstress.

The queen smiles at her. "Of course not, dear," she says gently. "Men never believe what women tell them. That is why, when the dust settles and the blood dries, we are victorious."

When the queen was still the princess of another land, before she was sold for half the territory and gold enough to fund three wars, she prayed for the strength to survive.

A goddess answered—but it was not the goddess to whom she had prayed.

"Do you know me, daughter?" the Pale Crone asked.

"Yes," she murmured, lowering all the way to the ground, her forehead touching the dirt.

"Rise," the Pale Crone said, one finger touching the princess's hair. "Rise and know the greatest truth."

She rose to her full height, beneath a dark moon, and she smiled the Pale Crone's smile.

There is a queen wed to a king in a distant land. The king wages war against all of his neighbors but one. For that one, he need only wait; his father-in-law is growing old. His brother-in-law is weak-willed and flighty. *Like a woman*, he laughs with his council.

His wife hears him. She shares a glance with her dark handmaiden, a pale smile hidden on both their lips.

The Pale Crone has a Dark Sister.

Their elder sister, prayed to by most as the Great Mother, tells them, "This is a dangerous game you play. My husband grows impatient."

The Pale Crone cackles. "Is that not like a man?" She and her Dark Sister share a smile.

"It is a dangerous game," the Dark Sister agrees, blood on her teeth. "But we play to win."

The king wages war on multiple fronts, and his gold grows low. The people are unhappy—their brothers and their sons and their husbands come home in fewer numbers all the time.

The queen prays on a moonless night, her dark handmaiden beside her, and she rises with the shadow of blood and the Pale Crone's smile on her lips.

Patriarch

He eats the first out of self-preservation,
the second through fifth out of fear,
and the sixth out of spite towards
his wife's determination to have a child.

When the young god comes, tall and golden,
he watches in awe until the blade falls.

After Troy

I. Andromache

You shimmer still, Helen, the ash of Troy
at last faded from your skin—did with it
fade your sin? The stench of guilt for our boys
followed to your throne where you still sit.

Invite me in, dear sister, wife to my
husband's brother. Invite me in as an
honored guest at your table, eye-to-eye.
Ten years on those walls we stood hand-in-hand.

You held my son in his first minutes of
life; you delighted in his innocent
smiles. You remember, sister, my dear dove?
My light, my darling boy, son of a prince—

I will never see my baby tall and
strong, bright as his father. I will never
again kiss his brow, my son or my man.
Glimmering Helen, your throat I'd sever

should I ever again sit across from
you at your table. Invite me, I dare.
But for my anger I would long be numb,
and to scorching rage, I have been laid bare.

II. Helen

Andromache, you call me sister to shame me,
      believe I do not grieve
the
   fall
of the beautiful city that felt more like   home
than ever did Sparta.

Andromache, I am not blameless for
    the tragedy   the desecration
             the blood—
I confess this openly and with a willing heart.
I hold my blame,   and my guilt,   and my grief,
cling tightly to it. I would let it all d r o w n me—

But Andromache, who remains with memories of
    your son's laughter
        save the two of us?
   I mourn   and   in that mourning
       immortalize
the   m a j e s t y
of Troy
as it was.

Andromache, you call me sister
and seek to   wound me.
I tell you now, that title is
       all
I would claim for myself,
standing together with you atop
the mighty walls of our beloved Troy.

Gifting

listen the wind whispers. *look* murmurs the sun. *feel* urge the rocks underfoot.

smooth against her fingers, the jar gleams enchantingly in the afternoon's light.

within it, something sings; clever, pale fingers play across the mouth of the jar, where a golden stopper rests.

a gift from Zeus himself, this jar, with a great prize inside.

watch this, ordered her husband, placing the jar in her hands. *keep it safe. never open it—because my brother says.*

she herself, holding the jar, is a gift from Zeus, and she herself smiles, fingers around the stopper, pouring out what is inside.

Pomegranate Queen

    oh Persephone
for you we sing
flowers bloom to gentle rain
light glows from the deep
    as your story is told
        and   told
        and   told again
the world warms in bitter heat

pomegranate juice stains your skin
seeds dance across your fingers
the world starves
    oh Persephone
    queen of the dead

you were not tricked

    your story is told
             and told
                    and told again

our queen for whom we sing
    you were not tricked
no subterfuge keeps you in your realm
beloved queen

Sacrificial

oh, Mother, i see that the
winds have stilled and
Achilles does not wait
for me—you scream and
clutch for me but Father's
hand on my arm, strong and
sure, guides me to the alter. oh,
Mother, i know i have told
you of the dream that returns
to my sleep every month with
the swelling of the moon. you
scream for me, Mother, i hear
you. Father will not meet my
eyes and so i stare past him, to
the sky. Mother, i would tell
you not to fear or to mourn for
to the sky is where i will go
once Father has spilt my blood
to sate the rage of the Huntress.
i have dreamed of this moment,
when the wind awakens with
a roar upon my last gasp and i
forgive Father, Mother. i do. this
moment, when a princess dies
so that a war can begin, is what i
was born for. i forgive every soul
who guided the way, and i look
from the sky to you, Mother,
when the knife in Father's
steady hand bleeds me.
i have dreamed of this moment,
my one and only taste of glory—
you are silent, Mother, as to the
sky i return my darkening gaze.
i would tell you not to mourn
but the Huntress has clasped my

hand and pulled me to the sky,
wind roaring in my ears with the
baying of the hounds, and laughing,
fleet-footed, i follow the goddess.

Wanderer

She spends a year in Vienna, another in Rome, a year and a half in London, six months in Paris, eight in Tokyo—she travels to every major city, to all the marvels, to the greatest libraries and museums of Earth. She roams the Amazon, the Serengeti, the Outback. She sees new faces, learns new names, lives a different life every day for a year.

You will never have a home, never have a people, the god she rejected proclaimed, head held regally high, voice ringing out against the stone. *Wander until you die, ageless and unknown, and then wander in the afterlife.*

She kept her eyes on the ground, but her spine straight and her fists unclenched. Her father, the only priest left to honor their god, had gasped and her mother had wept. But her own eyes were dry then and have remained dry still.

However, the god added, *should you come to realize your error, say my name and I'll return to you. When you become mine, the curse shall be lifted.*

She held her tongue instead of promising, *That will never happen.*

And so she wanders, with no people and no land to call her own. She has no responsibilities, no duties, no expectations.

She never even thinks the god's name, for there is so much to do, so much to see.

She laughs as the sun rises on another day, thinking, *Thank you for the curse.* Today, she is in San Francisco, and there is a whale-watch tour waiting for her to join, ocean air for her to breathe, another life to step into.

Reign

Rex, they call him, the killer of kings
who takes the crown, the throne,
the place in the queen's bed,
the favored son, blessed by the gods,
father of a new dynasty,
ushering in the most glorious of days.

Rex, they call him—
Until he learns his own father's name.

Shoulders

On the other side of the horizon, where no man
has walked, there is a mountain without a name that
any man knows, and on that mountain there stands a
god forgotten, a god who still holds the weight of
the world on aching shoulders, a god with a broken
back yet who refuses to break because when he trembles
canyons gape, and when he shifts waves swallow cities; and
though the gods who placed the world on his weary
shoulders are long gone, he still remains—And he will
hold the world until even he is dust, on the
other side of the horizon where no man has walked.

why
ask the children
why hold the world?

because
the god answers
you live to ask

Shadows Eternal

Once, they had loved her, the lady of the night. They gave her offerings of fruit and flowers, of songs and music, of dancing. Once, they sacrificed to her those with the greatest potential and her people grew ever more powerful, in the midnight shadows.

But then a new god came to their shores, blown in by a warm westward wind.

Why worship the dark when light is blooming? Why indeed.

But she is not jealous. She does not mourn. When the light fades, the dark still waits, patient. Eternal. For every dawn, there is a dusk—and for every dusk, a dawn.

The new god is greedy. So incredibly young. He shines brightly... and his fire consumes nations, salivates over bloodlines, burns until there is nothing left. And then he moves on, converting the next and the next and the next.

The ground is still fertile. She comes in the night to run her fingers through the ashes; there is still life in the dirt. It needs but a song to begin anew.

Once, they worshipped her with songs. The new god has no time for music.

She is patient. What burns brightly eventually fades away. The shadows always wait.

Rubies & Roses

Hunger

When, hand-in-hand, they walk
out of the woods, stench of smoke
lingering with each breath, taste
of burnt sugar on their tongues, they
say nothing—eyes speaking to each other
through a glance in the moonlight, they both
see the endless hunger growing, gnawing
at the back of two throats.

Dreamer

She gazes out the window, chores undone,
our dreamer of a sister,
the youngest, the loveliest,
the laziest of bones.
Our father dotes, Mama long gone—

The two of us, not much older,
must see that things move along. I,
the oldest, handle the farmland, helped by
my husband-to-be; I, the second, handle the
gardens and fix up the house as
needed, helped by my sweetheart and neighbor
boys, who accept their payment in pastries.

And she, our little sister, is to clean
the house and cook the meals but usually
she sits with our father by the fire
and they tell tales from morn to eve.

Father, who once worked ceaselessly
to give us a better life than his and Mama's,
now wastes days away, and we implore
our sister to take her duties in hand.
But instead she gazes out the window and
tells Father of the prince who will surely
one day take her away to a life so grand.

Ocean Calling

Come, come, boy, sit wit' me, listen to an old man's tale. Once 'pon a time, here in our very own village by the sea, a strappin' young man went a'walkin' along the shore. He was a fisherman 'n a fisherman's son 'n a fisherman's grandson, spent most his life on the water, so he knew well the legends of the ocean and those what dwelled there.

So'n that strappin' young man saw the fur bundled 'neath the rocks, he knew true what he'd found. 'a'cause in those days, there were selkies, people with two skins. They could take off their seal-skin, the one for the water, and walk on two legs as if they were landfolk like you and me, more beautiful than any human woman you ever seen. Their men are mighty fine, too, but we're not here to talk 'bout the men.

The fisherman knew that he'd never'n find a more beautiful bride than a selkie wife, so you can be sure'n he took up that bundled fur and hid it away.

That night, a woman, prettier than any you ever seen, she knocked on every door of every house out by the bluffs. None o'em could say they'd found a fur coat (that's what she called it, 'a'course, but all o'em knew what she was looking for; as I said, selkies were common in those days) until the last door she knocked on. Then, the fisherman opened the door and he told her that he'd destroy the fur if she didn't become his wife and give him sons.

What could she do but agree? Yes, I'm sure you're more clever than the fisherman by a far sight, wouldn't ask for such a curse. Hush, boy, just but listen and you'll learn.

It was a small wedding since the fisherman's parents were long dead and his sisters all gone to live with their husbands' families. The selkie cooked 'n' cleaned, gave the fisherman two boys and a girl. She gossiped with the neighbors and attended church on Sundays and raised her children 'til the sons were big enough to go out on the water. Her daughter, she kept home with her.

Years passed. Years and years and years, all while she cooked and cleaned and f—well, you know. Always, through it all, she listened to the sea, searchin' everywhere she could imagine a man might hide a fur.

Everyone knew what the fisherman's wife was, 'a'course. She was too beautiful 'n be landborn. Her daughter, that girl was just as beautiful, or she would be, one day, once she'd grown into herself. But no one spoke of what they knew, and no one ever acknowledged that she once knocked on their door looking for a fur.

Whenever the fisherman went down to the tavern, yes, this very place, he'd talk to all the fellows about his wife and how perfect his'n life was, how he'd found himself the perfect little wife. His friends complained (ach, they complained!) 'bout natterin' wives and children underfoot, 'bout the tax collector and the wild sea, but that fisherman, he just smiled 'a'cause since he'd hidden that fur, the sun smiled on him and nothin' could go wrong.

That's the magic, you see? And that's the curse.

Because the seaborn 't'ain't like the landborn, and the fisherman never thought to move the fur after hidin' it, all those years before. And when the location slipped his mind, he didn't think 'a'worryin' 'bout it. By then, his wife was nursin' their first son with their second growin' in her belly, and she did everythin' he said without hesitation or complaint.

What more could he want? What more indeed.

Aye, but didn't his sons grow tall and his daughter fair, and his wife searched for her fur every day he went to the sea.

His wife, she didn't find the fur, though. Their daughter did. That girl-child found the fur in a box made of shell and stone, and she brushed her fingers through the thick, soft hair, fresh as the day her mother took it off to visit with her family as women. The daughter didn't know what it was, 'cept beautiful, so she took it on home to her mama.

Don't you argue with me, boy! Just listen. Ach, you young ones...

Anyhows, the closer the fur came to her, the louder the sea roared, until she stood in the door to her husband's house and watched her daughter walk up the path, the fur around her shoulders like a cloak, excited because it was the most luxurious thing she'd ever seen, much less'n touched.

The fisherman's wife did not slip into the fur, not yet. But she hid it again, her daughter watching, and then her daughter asked, "Mama, why is the sea so loud?"

She looked into her daughter's eyes and said, "Child, it's time you knew the truth."

While the fisherman and his sons fished in the deep water, his wife told her daughter about the sea, the fur on her shoulders, the long years of watchin' the tide and yearnin', 'memberin', plannin'.

Oh, yes, she had planned. And now with her fur finally back in hand...

The daughter had always loved swimming, always dreamed o'the sea, so she asked, "Will you take me with you?"

"'a'course," said her mother, "if you want to come home to the sea."

That night, the fisherman and his sons trumped into the house with great joy; they'd caught a surplus of fish, enough to save 'til the end of the season and some to sell for extra coin. The wife and daughter had a feast already prepared, and the sister laughed with her brothers while the fisherman kissed and kissed his wife. All was well. All were happy.

The wife was the last to bed and she blew out the candle with a smile.

Now, what comes next, my own mama's mama saw. She was the healer the younger son ran for, when the boys found their father bloody and still, their mother and sister gone. She was the one who found the knife, still wet with salty water and sticking out of the fisherman's tore-up throat.

Those what remembered the young woman knockin' on doors understood; they'n knew exactly what done happen'd. The sons, 'a'course, those boys had no idea a'tall. The priest took them in, and they kept on a'fishing out on the deep water. Nobody could be sure what went on that night, but they say the fisherman's wife and daughter walked into the waves, and the selkie bride put her fur 'bout her shoulders and sang the magic to give fur to her daughter, and they swam and swam until our village was naught but a bad dream half remembered in the light.

But no one knows.

They say, though, that no man in our here village ever again stole a fur, and the fisherman's sons always watched the waves, hoping for their ma and sister to return.

They never did, and that's a fact. The sons married and had children, and they fished the deep water, and they grew old, 'n' they died, but the fisherman's wife and her daughter never set foot on our shore again. At least'n, that's what my mama mama's said, and she ought know.

Stepsister

You sawed off your heel
to fit your foot in
the slipper. What exactly did
you expect when you got
to the palace and had
to take off the shoe?

Bargaining

The child grows in her womb. Her
husband clothes her in the gold she
did not spin. Her lie echoes down
the stone halls and elaborate walls. She
dreads his return, the odd little man,
and the truth revealed by his demand.

Little Red

They all want the story. She gets dozens of requests for interviews, piles of letters, emails—two movies are in the works, and publishers and agents are all in line for her memoir. When she was on the stand, she didn't talk about it, or to the lawyer her parents spent the last of their money on, or to the psychologists she was sent to, or to the reporters who shouted variations of the same questions. She won't even talk about it to her cellmate, or to her ward-mates before that, or to her partner even before that, the darling man who truly loved her and bled himself dry to prove it.

She'll talk about anything except what the world wants to hear from her.

But in the privacy of her own mind, when the lights are out and she isn't tired enough to sleep, she thinks back to that day. It was the catalyst, the expert witnesses all said. Finding her grandmother's body, being attacked by a rabid wolf, surviving only because of a kind passerby. Because of that day, she shoplifted at twelve. Broke into neighborhood homes at fourteen. Carjacked at sixteen.

Her first confirmed kill is a neighborhood boy at seventeen. His death had been ruled an accident—until everything comes spilling out.

Spilling out, she laughs in her bunk in the dark. Spilling out like blood, like tears, like begging.

Everyone wants the story. Her parents have been vilified. The man who once saved her life. Even her late grandmother. Everyone has been blamed—she is simply too charming, too beautiful to be given death; instead, she's locked away for the rest of her days, the smiling Little Red who left a trail of blood from one ocean to another. She killed acquaintances and strangers, men and women, young and old. Stabbing, mostly, with a hunting knife, like the kind that saved her life years ago. Fifteen bodies, spread across fourteen states—sixteen, when the neighbor boy is added.

She laughs, staring up at the ceiling, trapped for the rest of her life. She laughs because unless she finally tells the story, her first kill will never be attributed to her.

Curséd

The meadow
       flowers
   blooms
Petals f
       a
          l
            l
     s c a t t e r
Wind wrenches the seeds
                                      away
                Barren
            Fallow
      Salt
   sinks
into the earth

Curses take root
       Flower
         Bloom
     Linger d
            e
                e
                   p
  Linger   l   o   n   g

The field—
   Bones rest in the dirt
   Petals flutter
      Fall
      Fallow earth
        Devours—
                —endures

The Tragedy of Snow White, in 7 Acts

I
her threadbare flats shredded
                         fall off her feet
she keeps running
         bloody prints left
                 on the floor in her wake
feet so numb she does
             not feel the pain

II
She lights the candle,
creeps quietly up the stairs.
Shadows loom, following, growling,
the shack as cold as the forest.
The dot of brightness fades
with every corner she takes
on trembling legs and bleeding feet.

III
see that? points one

     what? who? asks two

         intruder! yelps three

            four asks, what to do?

               five harrumphs

                   six giggles nervously

                       not again, seven sighs

IV
the huntsman returns at dusk,
ornate box dripping blood.
before Her Majesty, he bows,
horrific offering aloft in hand.

teeth sharp and white, she smiles.

the huntsman backs away without raising his head
and knows he will never taste freedom again.

V
An infant's dying sigh
Dust from a condemned man's grave
Seven drops of innocent tears
And seven drips from innocent blood

Stir together until it screams
Then, carefully dip the apple until
All the liquid soaks into the skin

VI
Luscious, gleaming in sunlight

Skin flush
Cool to the touch
As she takes it from the crone

The apple
Crisp in her teeth
Juicy on her tongue

VII
The queen, Her Magnificence, ever chill and solemn
from the winter wind she emerged,
sleeps well under thick and soft blankets
alone in her marital bed.
The skin of the apple glints in moonlight.
A young girl's skull, hung on the wall,
shimmers in the same.

Rubies & Roses

Give me a sip of water, dearie, the old witch croaks, but she's in a rush and sarcasm drips from her tongue like the water the old witch wants, and the old witch cackles and glows and changes, and now there's a beautiful fairy with glimmering wings gazing at her, ice in her eyes, and the beautiful fairy croons, *Oh, dearie, I know just what to do with you.*

She runs, she runs faster than she ever has, tripping along the path, but the fairy's laughter and the fairy's curse follow her. Of course they follow her.

No one can escape magic, especially not the evil (step)(half) sister of the tale.

I didn't know, she cries (a snake slithering out of her throat). Who knows they're the villain of the story?

Where do the cursed ones go? Who accepts them into the home, allows them to sit by the fire on a frozen winter night, offers them water and bread, lets them bathe and rest? *As we do for the least of these,* the woman of the house says piously, and her smile is only a little brittle when the cursed one gestures her thanks.

As the cursed one rises to her feet, one of the children rushes by, accidentally knocking into her; she gasps in shock and trips back, where her hand brushes against the hearth.

Could anyone have the strength of will to not scream when burned?

Screams of horror join her scream of pain, and the cursed one flees into the night, leaving only a dozen toads and frogs behind.

Terror is venomous snakes three feet long or less, anger non-venomous snakes of any length, shock enormous toads, and pain poisonous frogs.

But the happier emotions, the sweeter words? She doesn't know, for nothing like that comes out of her mouth anymore.

And the cursed one's (step)(half)sister? The blessed one, as those so gifted are called?

Oh, darling, the old witch chortles with the beautiful fairy's voice, *None of us give true blessings.*

When the prince demands her hand in marriage, she longs to decline, to run back into the woods, to the lovely little cottage she used to keep for her (step)mother and her (step)(half)sister, to the land she knows, the land that knows her, the ground she's sowed, the pond she's splashed in, the trees and bushes that saw her birthed and watched her grow.

But there is nowhere to return to, no home waiting.

Of course, Your Highness, she murmurs; two opals and three violet petals fall into her hands. As expected, she gives them to the attendant she can go nowhere without.

Everyone envies the peasant woman the prince weds on a bright spring morning. The beautiful woman (*barely a woman,* one courtier mutters to another, *more of a girl than anything,* because he has a daughter that age) weeps tears of joy throughout the ceremony, and with every tiny hitch of her voice, a pearl tumbles to the floor.

A sip of water, dearie? the old witch coughs.

Of course, Grandmother, the girl says, pulling the bucket up and using her own ladle to scoop some water.

You're a good girl, the old witch says, and in a flash of light, she becomes a beautiful fairy. *What reward would you like?*

The girl blinks at her. *Reward?* she asks. *For a sip of water?*

As she lays beside the snoring prince, silent tears running down her face, the blessed one remembers that there was no kindness in the beautiful fairy's eyes.

They Do Not Speak of After

They do not speak of after, when the simple
peasant girl must wear the finery of court and
play a game she never learned. // They do not
speak of after, when the wild girl-child who ran
through the woods freely chasing birds and plucking flowers
must be draped in jewels, still, silent, and never
speak her mind. // They do not speak of after,
when the maiden has been crowned queen, the power
she wielded once as a nobody out in the
world stolen from her along with every dream she
ever had of a joyful life of her own.

Advice to a Widower

Ten times a widower is a bit much—
The women 'round here so abhor your touch?

Wonder is not a fatal sin, my friend.
In future, away your spouse you should send.

Dark and Fair

Oh, Papa, she thought, *you have no idea what you wished for.*

Once upon a time, there was a princess pale as snow, red as blood, dark as a moonless night. A good girl, she always had a smile for the servants, a kind word for the knights, a wave to the commoners as her carriage drove past.

Once upon a time, there was a sorceress. She, too, was pale, was red, was dark. She, too, had a smile for the servants, words for the knights, a flick of the wrist for the commoners.

You don't think I'm talking about different people, do you? Oh, you poor dear.

The queen died in childbirth, after a hard pregnancy. Truthfully, though the healer would never say it, she should not have carried a child. *What will be will be,* the seer murmured, fingers trailing through the water. *What will be...*

The king named her after her mother: Marguerite. He called her Margery.

The king did not listen when the seer whispered, *Beware the name of the dead.* Of course he didn't.

Do kings ever listen?

Margery was a delightful child. She learned everything a princess should know, ever smiling. She visited the cooks whenever she had a moment, spent a stolen afternoon here and there with the hedgewitch, bowed to the priest's god when brought to the chapel. She could recite all the saints and throw together a charm to sweeten the meat before her twelfth summer.

No matter how much time she spent in the sun, her skin never darkened. Though she never painted her lips, they were always rouged. Her hair glinted ebony when any light shone on it. She was a beautiful girl and the king knew she'd be more beautiful still with every year that passed.

The king loved his daughter; too, he had married her mother for love. He wanted her to feel the joy he felt the first time he ever saw the queen.

A proclamation was sent throughout the continent and all the eligible sons flocked to the royal halls.

The king, of course, did not ask his daughter if she wanted to marry. It was her duty and so she would—for love or otherwise.

His name was Cole, the younger prince of the great southern isle, a good man; he would be a decent Prince Consort, when Margery ascended the throne. He would never be king, not of her realm.

He was a good man, with one great fault: he accepted things at face value. He would be a good figurehead, one of his friends thought, the overlooked son of a duke. Cole would be a good figurehead, indeed, after his wife, the queen, died in childbirth. It would be a long 18 years with Prince Consort Cole as regent before the child could inherit the throne.

Margery did not love Cole. But he was a good man and she had a duty to the realm.

When she survived the childbirth, the duke's son waited patiently to try something else.

The wrong person drank the poison and the only child of Queen Marguerite fell down dead.

Once upon a time, there was a princess, a lovely girl who grew into a lovelier woman. She was fair and she was just and she kept a calm head no matter what befell her. Her father, the king, died just before her twentieth year, a month after her wedding; it was a terrible accident, when the king's horse stumbled and the king landed on a stump. But the king's daughter, though she cried silently through the funeral procession and the coronation, never made a sound save when she swore to uphold the oaths of her bloodline and faithfully serve her realm.

The queen gave birth to a daughter; the Princess Magdalene died of poison before her fourth birthday. The queen miscarried what the seer said would be a son.

Through it all, though she wept, the queen never made a sound.

But then—the priest could not help her, and so she found a witch.

You have the potential, Majesty, the witch said. *But once you learn, you can never unknow.*

Queen Marguerite did not hesitate.

The duke's greedy son had an accident. Too did the prince consort. As did all the courtiers from the great southern isle.

The world is a dangerous place, my dear.

Queen Marguerite's hair is as dark as midnight, her lips red as blood, her skin pale as bone. Where there was once laughter in her heart, now there is only sorrow.

Look into the mirror, child. What do you see? You see a princess, do you not? Of course you do.

Once upon a time, so did she.

Oh, Papa, she thought, standing at his grave, apple in hand. *Why did you give me the name of the dead?*

Crying Wolf

A monster, the boy cries
A monster from the woods

The farmers, the blacksmith, all his
Neighbors—everyone runs to his aid

He laughs, the boy, at their faces
In annoyance they go back to work

A monster, the boy cries
A monster from the woods

They all come again, rough men he's known all his life
And they leave again, annoyance now anger

He laughs and returns to the field
Boredom sated for now

A monster, the boy cries
A monster from the woods

They come, angry when he laughs, and
With a thump to his ear, they stalk away

                     The monster slinks from the trees,
                        prowls around the field.
                  The sheep tremble, huddle close.

The boy shouts, *a monster*
A monster from the woods

Nobody comes as the boy watches the
Monster, eyes catching on the fangs, the claws
A monster, the boy screams
Nobody comes

The sheep wander home as the sun sets
The farmers, the blacksmith, the neighbors—

They notice not the silence until dawn
When no one comes for the sheep

That loathsome boy, they complain
In the field, they find no reason for his absence

> In the woods, the monster licks its lips,
> yawns, stretches every joint, each limb,
> and returns to its lair to curl up on a nest
> of bones and sleep for another year
> until hunger wakes it again.

A Fairy's Tale

13
How many fairies they invited to the christening

12
How many years they waited for a child

11
How many seconds of horrified silence before the queen screamed

10
How many months until the king's stupefied terror hardened into rage

9
How many guards accompanied the princess everywhere she went

8
How many times the princess tried to learn about the curse

7
How many tutors the king executed for giving in when the princess
    pled for the truth

6
How many times the queen begged the king to show his people mercy

5
How many times the king listened

4
How many wars the king nearly started as he sought a cure

3
How many fairies died when the queen wondered if magic might work instead of war

2
How many times the princess came within a hair's breadth of death

1
How many fairies it took to destroy a realm

0
How many breaths the princess takes in a rotted castle in the middle of a haunted wood

Fireplace

She misses the fireplace. She knew who she was there: Cinders, maid, servant, less than a toy, slave.

Now, with the world full of the unknown, she is never sure what is expected of her. She has a fleet of servants in her service and she hates commanding them. The food is extravagant yet tasteless, and she misses the simple broth of her own kitchen. The dresses stretch forever behind her and she can barely move in them.

She has no freedom here, in these sumptuous halls. Even when she was a penniless slave for her sisters, she had time to herself. Now all she has are the scant, dark hours of early morning, alone in her too-soft bed. She longingly thinks back, remembers the days before the ball.

This life does not compare. Cannot, for she is more of a slave than ever before with no escape remaining. Huddled beneath the silk covers on a bed that could hold a family in the most beautiful wing of the palace, she longs for the hard floor of the kitchen and the ash of the fireplace.

The magic ball with all its jewels disguised the truth. The handsome prince's beautiful blue eyes gleam cold by light of day. The queen spends hours daily molding her into aristocracy but they both know she will not survive.

The palace is stifling. Somber. For all its loveliness, it is not kind.

They call her the Lady Jocelyn, the princess of a forgotten land, last of a long-lost royal line. They can clothe her with the fanciest, most expensive dresses of the kingdom. She can say the lines they give her and smile—But she is not Jocelyn and everyone knows it. She is Cinders, the maid from the fireplace, her fingers stained with soot, her hair limp, dull. She looks in the mirror and sees her world as it was, before the ball and the dance and the stroke of midnight. Her godmother no longer answers her calls. Her stepsisters have wed above their station. Her stepmother kisses her cheek when they see each other, eyes shining with glee.

She wakes into a nightmare every day and she's falling ever farther into the web. She cannot see a way out.

In the scant, dark hours of the morning, she knows there is none.

This is what she dreamed of, curled up near the cooling hearth. She longed for this. Now she has it. She will be queen and yet still a slave—always a slave. Only her attire and name have changed; she is who she always has been, silent and bright Cinders, except instead of a drab shift she wears shining gowns and instead of a cold stone floor she sleeps on the third softest bed in the land. She rarely talks and to hear her laugh is even rarer. She smiles and nods and curtsies. She dines and dances and demurely sits beside the prince. Her prince. Her betrothed. *Hers*—but not. Nothing in the world is for her, in this cage encrusted with rubies and pearls, gilded with flowers and courtiers.

In her mirror, she sees the world that was. She sees the girl she still is, a lovely portrait painted in finery. Her fingers are heavy with rings, her neck with elegant chains. Her dress drapes over her, full of history, and always eyes watch, judging, damning.

A slave to a queen, yet still a slave—beautiful, fragile, pale with powder, still stained by the light of the sun. Her hair is washed and brushed each day; it shines golden beneath the thin circlet placed on her head when she leaves her room. Her eyes are ringed with paint until they seem to almost leap off her face, luminous and lovely.

Only she knows they're dull compared to how they used to be.

They make an attractive couple, she and the prince. When they dance, she remembers that first time, how exhilarating, how fun, how it felt to be held in the prince's arms. But she looks into his eyes now and sees him for the man he is: cold, aloof, spoiled. He will not be a fair ruler nor a king beloved by his people. She looks in his eyes and leans against his chest, caught in a web she can never escape, and she misses the stone floor in front of the fireplace.

She will become queen. The circlet on her head crushes her with its weight and her gorgeous green dress constricts around her. The light chains pressed against her throat freeze her skin. His eyes are even colder. The people on the streets call her his beloved, but those who live in the palace know: She will always be the girl from the fireplace, young and innocent Cinders, even when she rules as Queen Jocelyn.

She dreads the wedding night and his arms tighten around her. They keep dancing, whirling and twirling, appearing a couple fully enthralled with each other. She gazes at him and longs to shudder at his touch. The ball will end and the wedding looms and she is a fly trapped in a spider's elegant web.

She is beautiful, as is he, and their children will be more beautiful still. The citizens love her now but when he ascends the throne, she will be hated.

He presses a kiss to her forehead and she prays that she wakes in the kitchen, having never attended that ball.

Escapism

She watches the sun
                rise
She watches the sun
                set
Another day trapped
   Hoping
       waiting
              wishing
Another day
       wanting

She watches the moon
                And the stars
                        And the birds

She imagines freedom
   Though she doesn't know the word

She watches the sun
                the moon
                        counts the turns

                She is too high to survive a jump
                The wall is too shear to grip

She watches the sun
                the moon
                      counts the turns

Blankets
    Shirts
        skirts
            underclothes
                Hair so long it aches
A dozen knots to keep it all in place

Bemused
    why did you not wait?
Scoffing
    i waited long enough

To the Sea

What was his name?
her sisters cry as she fades away,
and the last thing she hears is
    Was he worth this price?
and the last thing she thinks is
    Oh, but he wasn't.

The Twilight Kingdom

Everything is frozen at the exact moment the curse fell—water being poured into mugs, servants setting platters down, a dog's tail mid-wag, a cat halfway onto a cushion. From the castle, it spread to the town, everyone going about their lives, forever mid-step: Horses never moving, children underfoot in the kitchen, a whip just hitting the back of a criminal and never leaving.

The surrounding forest is the same. Everything within 50 leagues of the castle will never again move, or age, or die. Should the curse ever be broken, life will continue on.

Of course... well. She learned from her sister's failure. There are no loopholes here.

Henry knows the story as well as anyone. The king was punished for insulting a fairy (no one ever thinks her name, much less says it aloud) and the capitol cursed into—something. It's not like anyone who saw it got out to tell. After half a century of the citizens trying to govern themselves, the three bordering countries annexed them. Da says there was mostly relief, after that. Finally there was someone in charge, even if one of them had been an enemy before the king insulted the fairy.

Most people moved away from the former capitol and its eerie stillness. No one ever went close anymore, avoiding it like the plague, and maybe they *got* the plague. That might've been the curse.

But Da is the loremaster, appointed by their new king, and he has to record what happened. So he and Henry (to carry the bags) go back towards the former capitol. They know the boundary of the curse because it is spring everywhere but the capitol's woods.

"Don't go in, son," Da says, sketching one of the cursed trees into the official tablet.

It has been autumn for nearly a hundred years here.

That night, Henry cannot sleep. Da's slumbering easily, but Henry is thinking about curses. Curses can be broken. How many people are trapped in the twilight? Every curse can be broken by the proper hero.

The next morning, Thom wakes up and his son is nowhere in sight. "Henry!" he calls. Not yet worried. Henry is fifteen and probably exploring. There are no predators around here anymore, and no one foolish enough to venture this close to the curse.

By mid-morning, Thom *is* worried. Where is his son?

He turns a horrified gaze towards the cursed woods. Surely not...

But there he is: Henry, mid-stride in the closest boundary of the curse. "Henry!" Thom shouts, running towards him and then stopping at the very last moment possible, nearly falling forwards into the curse. "Henry!"

Thom sobs into his hands. It is nearly a full hour before he controls himself, coming up and discarding ideas, pacing around, shouting at the sky and his son and the fairy and the king who angered her. He cannot leave here without Henry, but what of Meghan and Khora, back home? If he stays with his son, what will become of his wife and daughter?

Awake all night, he finally, at dawn, decides to try. He has his walking staff, a shepherd's crook, though they have not kept sheep since being annexed. He carefully pokes the staff over the border, keeping his feet and hands away as well he can, trying to hook Henry's arm. But however he angles it, it never catches, and he finally fumbles it. The staff lands all the way in.

He begins to cry again, falling to his knees. "Oh, my boy, my boy," he weeps, "Henry, you stupid boy."

He cannot stay. He gathers up a few supplies and the tablet, and returns to the king with a warning.

King Haralda takes the warning to heart and orders a great wall built around the capitol of a realm that no longer exists.

Thom goes home to his wife and daughter, and never forgives himself.

(In four centuries' time, the wall crumbles. A fairy's anger is vicious but *can* wane. Henry stumbles forward, the whip stings the criminal's back, the horses trot, the cat lands, the dog's tail hits the servant setting down the plate.

The curse is still a punishment, though—how can a king be a king without a kingdom? The world has moved on as leaves finally fall.)

Petals and Jewels

She wakes in the morning
>	Diamonds on her chest
>	Thorns digging into her breast
>	Petals caressing where she bleeds

She cries for her father
>	Rubies and emeralds against her fingers instead of tears

She prays to the fairies for deliverance
>	Amethyst cold on her tongue
>	Roses taste of ash

Oh but her sister was cursed
Everyone knows it
Just as everyone knows she is blessed
>	She speaks in gems and flowers
>	She'll never want for a thing
>	Men beg for her hand and her bed
>>		(her bed where the petals and jewels rest)

She whispers
>	A single sapphire falls for every word
>	She catches tulips in her palms

Oh but how she wishes
>	She had never gone to that well

Ignite

> *she strikes the match.*

A cold night, like all the others.
Sent out, in rags and bruises, to scavenge,
to forage—*Not enough*, he always snarls.
Bring more. More coin, more silver and
more gold. More pride spent for his
pockets, more blood frozen in her flesh.
More for him, none for her. The way of things.
She's tired evermore. No warmth, no light,
selling matches for pennies
to line pockets she never sees.

> *another lit, dazzling, small heat*
> *cupped in her hand. most beautiful thing*
> *she's ever seen. another. and another.*

Snow falling. His hands will bruise
and break. So cold, hidden in the corner,
frost on her fingers in fingerless gloves,
frost on her toes in raggedy shoes.
She is tired and hungry, hands pressed
against her belly, and the snow, the snow—
if she closes her eyes and imagines, butterflies
alight on her, so warm in the sunlight.

More, he demands, ever more. One
match at a time, and it is never enough. She
studies the little sticks in her hand as
the wind roars, biting her
bonedeep and all the way through.

*heat, only a strike away. huddled
in the corner, watching the rich
folk hurry past, she summons the
tiny fire again. again, a meager
fortune burns in her hands. again.*

The stars brightly gleam, the lamps
and the candles, the ovens and hearths.
She sinks to the snow, back against brick,
and she imagines that she can feel the sun.

*she strikes the match, the burn against
her fingers surging through her veins to
her heart, and it is warm, so
warm, burning, scorching, the heat of summer—*

They find her in the morning,
the tiny, bedraggled child,
spent matches around her,
and they tut and they pray
and they rant about the
state of the world when children
with nowhere to go freeze in the night.

That very same eve,
another girl is sent out
wearing rags and bruises
to sell matches that no one buys.

The Truth of Fairies

The difference between a *good* fairy and an *evil* fairy is in the ending.

Once, as the legends tell, there was a fairy who went uninvited to a royal christening. She cursed the babe and the land for a century—and then all was forgotten, after she sated her rage. Another legend tells of a fairy who tested a prince and cursed him when he failed; still another speaks of two sisters, one gifted with jewels falling from her lips and the other cursed with toads.
Tell me—which is good and which is evil?

There are always maidens wishing to go to the ball. Sometimes, they are peasants, born of peasants; sometimes, they are noblemen's daughters who fell on hard times. Occasionally, there is magic.
Her name is Lucinda, the lovely young maiden crying in the garden. She has but one stepsister, who is equally beautiful; her stepmother is not unusually cruel. But her stepmother knows that Yvette will already have ample competition for the eye of the prince, and Lucinda has been but a servant in the house for most of a decade now.

What good fairies do not mention is the price of magic.

Lucinda weeps in the garden, wishing with all her heart—
And then the fairy appears, gleaming and glimmering, to make all her dreams come true.

One legend mentions midnight, when the magic will fade away.
Lucinda is not so warned, for her story has a different end.
She rides in a carriage that was once a pumpkin, pulled by horses that once were mice, driven by a man who was a lizard, in the most gorgeous gown she's ever seen that was once rags hanging off her. She enters the ball breathlessly, gazing about in wonder, and

perhaps it is her innate beauty that catches the gaze of the prince. Or maybe it is the magic.

Either way, they dance. He dances with none other for three hours. Lucinda sees her stepmother scowling, sees Yvette dancing with a smile, and she knows that tomorrow she'll still be a servant, and punished for this—

But for now, she dances in the arms of the prince.

The clock strikes midnight.
Magic has a price, even the *good* kind.

At first, Lucinda thinks only that her breath is caught because of the prince's eyes, gazing down at her in wonder. She has, after all, been dancing non-stop for hours. But her breath doesn't come back. She panics, gasping for air, clutching at the prince's arms, and once he realizes she cannot breathe, he shouts for healers.

In the garden Lucinda has tended since she was a child, a fairy smiles.

Wishes have power and another lovely young maiden's deepest wish has come true.

The fairy blows a kiss to the castle, gently strokes the newest ghost tethered to her, and takes flight.

What is the difference between a good fairy and an evil fairy?
Only how the story ends.

Exeunt

Deify

Tell me—
>You look for god (any will do)
>and what do you see?

Blood drips, blood drops,
the trap snaps shut,
bare your teeth,
snarl at god (any, all),
and swallow down
the burning ambrosia of the divine

Immerse yourself.
Consume as you are consumed.
Bend, break, reform,
(d)evolve
and tell me—
>How does your god taste?

ABOUT THE AUTHOR

Born and raised in Baton Rouge, LA, **Laura Williams** cannot remember a time she did not love to read; her passion for writing came later, but poetry has been her life-long love. The younger middle child of four, she has been blessed with a large, close-knit family. She earned her doctorate in education, focusing on adult literacy, in 2022 and lives with a mischievous cat.